i tulips

Mario Petrucci

i tulips

ENITHARMON PRESS

First published in 2010
by Enitharmon Press
26B Caversham Road
London NW5 2DU

www.enitharmon.co.uk

Distributed in the UK by
Central Books
99 Wallis Road
London E9 5LN

Distributed in the USA and Canada
by Dufour Editions Inc.
PO Box 7, Chester Springs
PA 19425, USA

ISBN 978-1-904634-93-5

British Library Cataloguing-in-Publication Data.
A catalogue record for this book is available
from the British Library.

Typeset in Albertina by Libanus Press
and printed in England by
Antony Rowe Ltd

ACKNOWLEDGEMENTS

I am grateful to the Royal Literary Fund for supporting my Project Fellowship entitled *Writing ↔ Science*, and to the Arts Council England (London) 'Grants for the Arts – Individuals (Lottery)' Fund. Thanks are also due to the editors of the following publications and web sites where versions of some of these poems first appeared: *Acumen, Envoi, Feeling the Pressure: Poetry and Science of Climate Change* (British Council, 2008), *Interdisciplinary Science Reviews, Into the Further Reaches* (PS Avalon, 2007), *The London Magazine, The Loop, Life Lines: Poets for Oxfam* (Oxfam CD, 2006), *Magma*, nthposition.com, *Oxford Poetry, Poetry Express* (survivorspoetry.com), *Poetry Salzburg Review*, poetrybay.com, *Stand, Swarm* (Beehive Poets: Wellhouse, 2008), *Trespass, Under the Radar*.

A recording of a portion of this collection was lodged with the British Library Sound Archive in July 2009 as part of the *Archive of the Now*. *how does, what happens between* and *a half hour after* were broadcast by BBC Radio 3 in its 'Poems for Today' series. *tulip, sanctuary of* and *i rather love* are reproduced from *somewhere is january* (Perdika Editions 7, 2007). *in hay waist-deep was* was a runner up in the 2008 Academi Cardiff International Poetry Competition and was broadcast on Resonance FM (with *everyone begins as fish &*). It was also included in *Poetry : the Environment*, an online educational resource commissioned in 2008 by the Poetry Society (www.mariopetrucci.com/ ecology.htm); *today i could go* appeared in *The Green Poetry Pack*, another part of that same commission. *one pink heart* was commended in the 2008 Poetry on the Lake Competition.

I should add, as context, that this volume is a selection from the first 400 poems of the ongoing *i tulips* sequence.

My appreciation to Martyn Crucefix and Jacqui Rowe for such honest response. Finally, to Brennos and Annie, all I can demonstrate here is the inadequacy of acknowledgements sections.

Cover image: *tulips* (2007); author's artwork, acrylic on board.

CONTENTS

Tulips

for Annie

'. . . and the long stem of connection'

Denise Levertov

Tulips

That
tulip set
by the window

in its vase
of dusk is like
a flame. You

cannot help
but say – *no.*
Because a

tulip caught in
that glass *is*
a flame –

and once you
have said it how
to return to

bloomed stem
or soft spike
of anther

where now
is fire? Words
burn – bridge

colours away
from colour – so
while one

tulip flares
we lay waste
to night and

glimpse
our reddened
names – the way

Anne
cannot bear to
end – or as you

take your leave
of Mario that
ah

so missed and
strange. And you
sputter so

fierce with it
that you say it
again –

that this gift of
tulip is un-
like any

other – which
fires my lips
with a glow

already half-
subsiding as you
turn to gaze – to

look with a mind
on the very point
of opening.

i

'. . . these empty seconds
I fill with myself'

Amiri Baraka

a single drop can

musk a home –
roll up stairwells &
nudge through jackets

sad with draping then
shoulder past attic-
flap till in

rafter skirting
& weight-bearing
wall the whole house

slows to it – swells to that
one substance whose
clock-tick is im-

perfection & under
its surface an *ave* kneels
sucking my lifethread to a

point to thread endless
needles of silence &
i of a sudden am

very *of* – as if
these rooms had
matched me inner to

outer – as though
world & i had
made time

to sit to-
gether each
waiting for other

to speak

let us

talk
lip to lip as
though morning

just made us –
parted these
mouths

wan
as clay to
make way for

words that are
for us to
try

first
time on air
deft as dew on its

leaf – so let me
speak as an
adam

might
whose moment
is under a kind god

who looks on a half-
made garden
& come

eve
-ning will
change his mind

starlings so

ravenous at my apples
jump branches as
i might jump

ships – yet i
think myself apart
as they move in half-flight

contrast to static rounds of
flesh they are almost
as many as &

open up in bird-
tip shapes – in white
chevrons i can see from w-

here i stalk them adrift with en-
croachment till like them i
bear my weight

no longer : this
newtonian mass of
what i want – not that snake

of sight – but unpecked apples
so discrete they make
the other side

of frost into
festivity wherein i
cradle one miraculous

apple much later than
the rest drawing
its noose of

wonder round
my table because it
sits in its middle so out

of season & thus a
proprium & so
do not let

starlings eat
but burst blackchaff
at my bullet-clap knowing

they think my hands a
thing of dread a
thing a

part & gone
in a swarm i am
left a tree cored of

starlings & cannot be
sure i was not
of them

i rather love

not things but
what lies behind
these the way a year

is sometimes glimpsed
past ear of corn or
december

come
out of blue to
one who knew only

sun – perhaps such
are best unsaid
so all might

speak of
corn & sky or
strip decembers

down to black-
scaffold
trees

where
life sings &
sings to death each

silenced thing

an old brood

mare   i
do not see head
low   as grass in her

field   of red & puce
ruminating &
slow   i

steer down
her rail   no horse
there   till   all-at-once

black bulk starts   this
edged vision   her
     canter

sudden as
finding the foal
deeper in her than any

she bore as i follow
one-eyed   down
into back-

most reach
of blood   that
field   she & i   stirred

today i could go

out to dress myself in
nature : these
annular

pupils
borrowing
fish-rings from

rivers so like them
i would ever
widen &

inner ear
little-boned &
oboe-keyed might

pilfer a leaf from
fugal trees or
skin

grow up
past low-flying
geese bumping qu-

ills to fledge answering
zephyr – or some
aroma full

of city
scribe its corner
in me or salt in its pans

be pepper & crust of me – oh
if each going out
were only

home
coming to its yard
or two of matter whose

dark & light meet in
me   & make
shade

what if climbing mountain is less

defying weight – more a matter
of placing one hand where
the other was as

rock face slips
beneath you – one thumb
-hold at a time – that all but holy

mass loaded with pleasure so
tender – precise –
practised as a

lover falling only
at your pace – meeting
metre with measure & going

down so you may imagine you
ascend – thrilling even to
your slight mis-

takes till at
last both quicken
into ease whose sum

-mit opens to cupping
gasp & parts for
uninterrupted

blue where
humble & lifted you
view in watering eyes how

desire made a whole
earth dive yet
kept you

where you were?

here in me

his knack
of charging each re-
sonant space conveying cat –

that hand firm down its back
a lip at the lip of its
animal bottle

blowing just
so to draw its tongue
-thick note while his scraps

of salami taken dandily by
fangs were original
platonic each

thin-boned
creature knew in the
marrow might be its last &

is that him now stepping
into me from dark
into dark

as my lover
under my palms lets
me bring her to that shape

becoming so easy as blood
purrs under our bonnet
of blood

sufficient
turning itself over
love by love – & his relief

behind it – that sole figure
flesh must come to &
in its finding

own

§

this light shows

through you as dusk
where you turn
addressing

addressed
by our window
as though you wore

gauze of being here
more lightly when
i yearn through

you for light
beyond you yet
i learn the firmest

sight can hold onto
tonight is that
shaping &

shaped-by
almost-here
fern-coloured

dress

half a year & It

shifts : as any body
must – its lust a
touch looser at

the jowl – that
middling crease of
brow deepened by an

added shade of dark –
a twosome creature
all but one yet s-

hunted through in
-cremental selves by
diet of said-&-done in

downward insistences
of time so slight as to
make all difference :

though to super-
impose what it was
then on what it is now

might draw a rasp at
shimmering blur of
change – at how

unkemptly our
lovely album pro
-gresses dust – or

put recent snaps side
by side to get them
wrong way round

thinking
love in halves
could grow a little

wise & young

everyone begins as fish &

ends so – spiralling after
egg (that other half of our
chains) & setting gills

in gristled knot that buds
legs as tadpoles do & blow-
hole ears halfway down

the back & low-set eye
alien as featherless chick –
ah we have peered into

that shared ovum whose
blasto-flesh runs its gauntlet
of fowl & fish so fused at

the tail nothing can be told
apart – is this why when i am
late i find in upstairs dark

you – on placenta duvet &
hunched round self as wom-
bed ones are? – as though

i had just returned from
all eternity to catch you
naked out sleepwalking

space without even
navel-twisted purpled
rope to hold you

how does

fragrance of sleep drift
this easily through

rooms – as though
your resting had keys to

every chamber whose
open doors i

cannot step
through – i lie

alert & breathe spare
room breath & in

my casing
form you warm &

close   who slumber
farther from sense than

how would i
know? – perhaps that

shape a world might
have or

a home
if it woke from sleep &

walked

between   as

each lot of
room is
breathed now

between us – or
as each
will break breath

willingly across its
supple back
to kiss : or that vow

i lifted tureen-heavy
& pre
-carious offered to

you who never did
ask – or
that time driving

through dark on the
verge of
irretractable words

when half of
forest
leapt to its other

as quantum
bolt
of stag

what happens between

breaths when you
sleep is neither
you nor you

sleeping but
something ships
do darker & deeper

than night they find
themselves in
straining

at the turn
the balanced in
-stant when prow

hangs & world
could go
either

with
next swell or
under as i ballast

you unseen &
hold   this
breath

when you come at

last to my bed   glide in
right   beside as
fuller half

of me & me
at that   moment so
awake   with fit of you

at the spine of me   so
precise   your
one ex

haling
draughting down
the knobbled glass of

my back   then you   steal
in   your black-ice
twin of me

slip you
in & stiff me with
what you are   brimming

my borders   my contour
exactly & all
going

gone
into you   so
when my window-glass

moults mould &
they   push in
the door

through
my hush to find
you there   for all intent the

content & form the *instead*
of me   they will avoid
still-open

eyes in eye
less sleep & believe
me when i said   you were each

pause before breath &
i now impostor
displaced

night entering

as you take it in
through lungs dark
by familiar dark whose

breath cuts its shape
one shade sharper
against black

sleep having
risen to you tame
as a carp but not for

me – slumber something
i must take tonight
at this remove

& breath :
yours a hint of
wheeze becoming all

but that of a child you
heave on the spot
towards Lethe

& high above
you now – those
words that flew bat

-sudden from my
cave into your
thinning light

the flitter of
black scissors i
put you amongst

the innocent caught out
on a crag   under
Furied birds

all driven
up beyond you
by this turning in

-ward so towering even
i who made them
must strain

dark for keening

behind the lines

– just as you might never
find some white-worn
tongue of soap

long fluffed
beneath basin – or
fine marks of particular

weight penned in their
margin near skip-
bottom or

one flake
falling deep in a
cwm between sheer-set

neighbours of pine – or
with morning still
dark that

word
barely spoken
to your sleeping ear

one black

curl – against your nape as
you face into
sleep

& i
fall to single-
rhythmed breath expressed

there – whose hairline shift
hains against worry
some thread

here within
– making love plain
for one who takes love in in

small degree – as that hook of
dark against your neck
foxed &

soft with
living takes a bearing
into dream & old fish i let it

reel me after

the world you

make plunging
in your breasts white
hills warmed by their own

red sun hair compiled of sea-
bladder strung &
spawned

with stones
waist wrapped about
by lambs pinked to frolic

the eye & as you centre
my room where
you are is

its open
window   until you
lunge embrace this world i

am with another   run for
mornings terrestrial
train   not to

miss the world

a half hour after

you leave some al-
most thing starts : your
mattress impression stops

holding its breath – begins
to relax & swivel-chair
where you tackled

laces adopts that
strained angle of the clerk
requiring confirmation – then

i see through softly shut door
a house of pointers : your
draped towel on its rail

& bone scissors left
half-open there as though
simple addition of water could

jerk them to life : not so strange
then that a house should re-
member you with each

pine surface & glass
ornament its own sextant
keen for your one star to float

these bricks by – to hoist white
rooms thinned to canvas
by your sea-smell & i

no less join them : this
richer matter becalmed yet
seeming your merest breeze

might cast me off

love sends itself flowers

and mails its single-stemmed
blood down the spinal telegraph all
petal and thorn and never signs the card

o i stand at the delivery ajar and won
-drous at my syncopating lobes as
rhythmloveswells down

there to the one old tune
– *work it out* head puffs *work it
out* : that pencil-biting maths of trouser

and gusset forged in the belly-furnace
those matching sets of differentials
yielding smaller-version

selves – such noble
illusions i have borne through
changeling vein – azilian sumerian

cretan egyptian navaho graeco-
roman : all the one difference
through china belgium to

meso-america i crossed
burning and spurned bridges and
crossed myself pons-pubis to pons-cranium

spanned with that smile i cannot put on
for she who gave speech in chocolate
-sized pieces gave speech me gave

speech you – o prometheus bind
me in my red room on this red mountain
bind me to tell through the liver each form

of love – for there is married love and married
love with a pillow and married love with
pillows for head and foot and

married love with the pillow between
and the woman with six children and pillow
and the man who has come to woman who has

a husband to ask for a pillow and three men
who seek the same married pillow
– these are the forms

whose words have quarrelled
with pillows between – for illusion
excels as i say its three words over and

out with a voiceprint computers can register
grimly – o love you have sent appeasing
flowers and that delivery tries every

address down my spine but
i grow closer in calculating who sends
am singling you out by elimination – can

nibble your edges o love – earlobe viced be
-tween my lips those fluttering hands
clamped at my brow your bracing

breath upon my instruments – i
have you a hatchling in my palm i have
you as you were when you began and soon

means to determine your flight – to release
when you suit me for i would go naked
though not through eden though not

in the head and so will take you while
you are going take you while you are going
fast take you three in a bed with knowing but

then what one-dressed what *what* thrusting luck
i can still peel you back to climb in be-
side myself to slide – yes slide in to

love full clothed

ii

'the only way not to leave is to go'

Frank O'Hara

sanctuary of

APHAIA — not only fluted
pillar but this
clutched

pink
in its crevice
with blood in the throat —

not the felled bolus against
headaches of gods
but

slumbering
woman-child feeling
stone through her back   not

booth   not caption   nor
flies rubbing hands
but

gaze
so patient these
foundations pull loose &

warp

★

cicadas

revving up
for sun let slip
an extra watt : how

one begets that
cheesegrater
or

-chestra
shifting in the ear
as sand through gears of

current & if i reel in
time i may hear
that half

-moment
hill sway & swell to
scratchy concord or sun turn

afternoon in yellow hands
– dust on hot flags
spun

dozy in
skirts of breeze
to spiral brief arms

galactic

★

whatever light left

here is blue intenser than
ink buoying pink
smudges who

drown daily for
pleasure in aegean
crinkled & reigned by

sharpness to deckle fore-
shores under full pal
-omino manes of

cloud – ah
too soon across
those blood-wheeled cha-

riots – but now
that feeling i may have
feigned some hand in this

flotsam salvage of brilliance un-
brindled by elements
(for shore is

where i first found feet cloven –
became throatsome with
words skimmed off

water & galloped
for sea to place where
light is a catch   the light

                                        presses

   ★

what stirs this is-

land? – humming through my
days as flowers in their
beds are bumbled or

borrowing that cr-
inkling ribbon-cirrus for
outcrops headless with ocean

where this head itself bobs on
hock from some three-
fingered hand held

out to africa – ah
my mountain was reared
quick as a child – rumination

that grumbles to collapse
houses & my night is
slow arousal from

sleepless light – yet in
hills loud with dark these
wings have fanned the hive &

my legs jointed & japanned in
death kept frantic survival
hollow & at bay &

i lean into all small
winds eye scale palp fun
-nelled to the roar that razed me

here to stream with seas on all
sides which etch me blue
till i cannot bear this

hourglass sac of self
i believe i am whose nape is
a sifting through of head to trunk

– thus do i disbar these sands for
keeping eyes wide falls to
ward dream &

even watch-
fullness must outstrip
time : itself outgrown to some

thing dreamt

★

friend take me

on – not as volumes
whose spines flex with con-
fusion or half-erected schools of

confession raised arcadian
around my cloisters to
fix half-minded

thought whose luke
-warm dinners & fasts
propel this small engine

through biography two-
thirds lived in
– see in

stead that in-
itiation each moment is
to the next: turning us with planetary

certainty to this evening – that
table – a sentence you put
to me as one might

a knife with th-
in intent – see us sat
down together across a plastic

moon merging with dusk our
words   deciphering stars
who change their

symbols as
stop by stop then in on-
rush they appear to our monkish

pair half-drowned in textless
marginalia down among
dregs to plant this

pallid strain of
vine — constellations
may shift in our watch: in

that long watching we choose
where what one needs
of friends

lies rest-
less to the eye &
tenuous

as the dark between

⋆

one sailing

i am – this steady light of boat
ruddered upward through
night by flame

as though sea
took to verticals so
a flicker might float &

as all creeps downward that
lone stub-mast draws
other sails to

steer by or
cast nets together &
strengthen prows on pitch like

hands prayered towards water –
my light-drop cable-hung
filling its cabin

: sight falling
upwards yet anchored
to pupil-dark at the heart

so do i light me
& watch me burn this
small measure of body to

choose what is done by its glare
before my white sliver
adrift with dark

sputters behind
far headlands bearing
one head with it – one match

head leant into the stroke
& on the shore that
statued face

vacating &
where the buddha
smile was buoyed this

slight curvature of space

*

i have a bay

in me
whose walls
gaze out fresh as

milk to draw a tongue
of ocean lapping –
where eye

levels
horizon to
raise the bowed &

one spireless geometry
ushers this body
to its cooler

shadow
where dusk
touches my dusk

as absent-minded
& slack as a
lover

whose
desire is
single flame

by which i see –
one candle
set & lit

for me

as it wakes me

dark through the house – that blue-crazed
flash photography

there – one jagged
runt of blue thick & blurry with possessed

intensity making a sparkplug on the brow
cypress gasps to in

upwards stubbings
of cigarillo as black slick with oxy-blue

fume casts my atom through its funnelled
Bessemer of chaos all

hubless as a burst-out
engine where night has chosen this torn-off

V of stone quick with blued daguerreotypes
of a village shedding

stacked megavolts to
hurt daytime green & brown through shat-

-tered swipes of cloud working up to what
i half step into – might

strike before i know
violet so intense as to forget itself & me

suddenly aware of metal – of possibility's
remotest in-a-second

strike i could be spur to
that rending downwards welding to ground

its long-gathered energies as first-sleet rain
unseen on leaves: a rice

-fall for this moment
passed across the gorge whose thousand

electric eyes at once sweep open just as
i see they were all

this while kept shut
conducting me back to blue-black

knuckles on a frame & in its
doorway a mind

half dressed

*

four cypress

someone aligned & tectonic earth
did not touch

my eye
wanders among the unthought things

undulated & undulating – gathering in
the odd ox-eye

as mosquitoes
skit our tabletop mahogany as though

it were a darkening pool

*

out on the terrace
you stand – the cypress do not

prevent you
relieving an idle itch in your crease

of jeans as if
you were not at all strange   how

familiarity
softens us to ourselves

*

the glass
you left behind –

scallop-edged with
lip-prints

i could see
the cypress through

that glass – no less
distorted &

your mouth
proscenium arch

with darkening
stick of light

a day like
this can pass

withstanding
that rousing green

tension – lipped
till twilight

delivers one
yellow square of

you your
shadow moves

across

*

it is not
quite dark

but it is
now – as though

i never
slept while moonless

stars
enamel my smooth inside

of skull
where i stand in this

view: an
egg watching you

hatch in
your sleep &

a dog
barking &

the dog
star

i i i

'. . . the third way, the arduous path of appearance'

Martin Heidegger
(via George Oppen)

for Denise Levertov

tulip

repeats as
if it were me
-rely one pouring

upwards to melt
light with
light

: others
shake loose
this pane squaring

on to one square
field – same
as sun

turns
up its yel-
low dial &

volumed glow
eases petals
apart

as many
-petalled pelvis
is eased by red birth

or womb could
split & leave
its black

& yellow
baby standing
alert – ready almost

to tell

wood where

each tree is
a sound soft-spoke

to unwheeled sky
perhaps

or passing
cloud – i would set

mind as
these trees: closeset &

filigree
like something once hubbed

& radial staked
out : taken root & grown past

its paring
having absorbed what heat

comes in to build a year-by-
year body

encompassing body: mind so
still in its s-

hell as to
be

detectable
barely   till my

tomb stone
deep in upward shadow

leaps upon
me like a child around my neck

for Robert Duncan

tree i

scramble through
bough from
branch

: man
downcast
with gravity

forever looking up
& climbing
down

: boy
upwards
goes – only

bare soles to
commend
to bark

to this
green wood
hand & foot along

twig he caterpillars
out to almost-
air sway-

heavy
as fruit to
look down on

balding crown he
never hoped
to be

struck so
among roots
stoking autumn

leaves whose smoke
boy smells &
starts

to cry

once you begin what

next – what – when you
take next step in all
trust & feel its

heel-to-toe
losing each pledge
with tarmac – or catch

boy in his pram with those
fresh-made lips jinxing
your eye with his

bright water
gaze as he lifts both
hands – little pope who

celebrates your coming
drooling into bib
streaked with

pragmatics   so
what when you re-
fuse that brighter water

in the body with all its
years & chemical
apparatus to

fall down
this street no
longer pacing its

flatness but circular
illusion of earth
only just put

there to
hold you as it
presses down never

failing in its pressing to
bring you chin-high
with a child or

yourself?

captivated – by that

board of chalky chemistry where
sir pullulated his easy
reversibilities :

each double-
ended arrow humping
some poor bridling of chloride or

sulphate into equilibria my head
equated with stills of two-
way jumping horses

& after that
my favourite jacket
always the reversible whose

outside-in shrug of shoulders
turned am to pm or versa
vice – but even

that boy gleaned
how a word taken back
could not but leave its silhouette &

though from biology i knew failing
raindrop has to make up-
wards eventually i

saw how a man
retracing steps is still
a going forward – or how

revisiting that mock-wrought gate
his unschooled boy backed
& forthed is only his

youngself coming
at him ever facefront – till
his thesedays arrows of exigency

or of love seem mainly one
way though there are
mornings

in me yet
more beginnings
than ends wherein i am p-

liable as evaporable surface
whose drop whose final
pop inaudible in

to vapour is
sufficient return & i
see sulphates & chlorides – these

molecules teeming – in tiny re-
versible jackets swivelling
before the mirror of

this way or that
– divided matter strung
togetheras joined up eyesawaiting

me decided

child had made

sketchbooks of its
parts – that family arch
in eyebrows perfected   the fat

bow of its lip bent all with finger
tip brush & as each part
acquiesced to

touch that touch
& its confidences welled
separately into places one is

advised not at length to inspect
till it became   the self
portrait child

that walked that
the whitening adult came
to one late autumn morning un

expectedly sunned with head
shock-full of paleness
temples clearing

to whiteness
of black acrylic being
scoured back to canvas   that

pink parting the hair where
in the long gallery of a
plate glass street

was caught
in reflection that
summary old-child ex

pression of face & self gone
disparate ways a face
witnessing in

glass its re-
cognition   that it
had always been   its owned

work   looked at

in hay waist-deep was

uncle who said he saw
lash of rain snap
upward viper-

sharp to bite
the coming-down
tail – another tending

eaves from top-notch ladder
felt on his back
drops

worse than
wasps to a sack
while wife with foot

hard on bottom rung
kept her face of
tinder – yet

another
watched brown
slick of cloud a few

metres up suck back its
centre like a seam
in the roasted

bean – till it
split with blue &
for an hour all air smelt

of coffee – last it came to
me   i said   once
i stood

in rain so
ferocious streams
front & back – down

shallow contour of
nipples & ravine
between each

half of arse –
met at my pizzle
till i knew to my balls

how it felt to piss like
Orion: i said this
happened –

but they
laughed & took out
scythes & said the hay was

dry enough

men

out
walking
these   sub

zero men collaring
winter like a pit
bull –

greycoat
faces   strides
syncopated & all-inner

space their features as
outer clenches
down

with ice
of ages early
darkening reveals

tepid seed of planet in
zealous & end
-lessly

furrowed
cold: aye very s-
pace condescends to

meet them coming
as evening g-
hosts of

lung they
ex-hale then step
into: white wraiths null

holds up then shreds as
it shall them:
hanging

men
who kick through
air their tread-by-tread tweed

carcases while word
-less solstice
accepts

that
dot dot d-
ash of warmth they

ebb

you stepped straight

up to me :
made all the blazing
mall a buzz beyond your

temples – my gaze a
lens with you its
focal plane

you
raised a ha-
-lf-said thing the way a s-

lighted father might
with jaws re-
collecting

sour cud of a
son – though just
this once i thought i

heard veins in that forming
sound stand proud &
younger than

your brow l-
eased to echelons
of time – cheeks crazing

blood through coming
back & did
that lip

half-move to
bare those same brown
teeth? – but as your sight your

word seemed to resolve in
mine a reddish jacket
rash from

the crowd
intervened – left me
with the simple space that

you had been

they come with

that arrhythmic half-
pulse of dark   up the path
they know   in the one missed

beat of night   never threatening
its heart   & every planet
soul misaligned

that hung
instant   only
chronic sleeplessness

thinks it might   with a rare
nod have   dreamt
they come

reaching
for a key they
cannot have   pause

at the door   put out
by where they
were sent

before
not quite tapping
that mouse-thud downstairs

for familiars past the foiled
edge of their almost
awakening   no

body hears

last night a spider

wove round the open rim
of bottled bleach &
slid in – & in

ritual light of
morning i poured him
– prettified christ of arachnids

with that white body & crossed
white legs & as he swirled
down to sample

hell on my be-
half i swore i recalled
deep in pitch – him out there

feeding & gliding his small
black scratching – an
abseiling

all legs
glazed from the kill to
ply my rim of ear until he

fell – & from edge of dream
i heard his silk sacs
crackling – i

guess that kind
of sound when in some
churn of sleep the black cream

is rising

(on the onset of tinnitus)

as though in the night

cosmos had threaded each
ear with wire to
loop me

sleepless
round one wry
note – morning brought

sense of threshold
having finally
stepped

over – as if
pause to desire milk
from the shop on its corner were

sudden event any pitched a-
tom could swivel
head & sc-

reech distant
tyres to – or this rust-
iron core of brain had drawn at

last lone needle of filing to its
white-sheet silence
& now

i remember
mother telling
there were those

in our line who had it
stronger– deeper—
as choral din

held at gates
of coda yet c-
lung on to as if

up there future were
mere breath were
sostenuto

to make us
hanker for what
comes after as though

hell were back-wash of
heaven not creeping
back up but

in

now there is something

ever at the back of it
– some whitish
rind i

have to attend to – or
that extra under
cinematic

trees who wanders in
half whistler
half

hissing between teeth –
or cicadas that
loom

each silk thread to
one grey matt
just as

eyes are closing till
half-mating with
brain

their *syrups-syrup*
sicken out of
sleep – oh

god i want it pure &
green again as it
never was :

that *tabula rasa* nature
would once in a
while sink

me in so i might faintly
smudge with
breath –

not this showing through
of yellow weave
to

silence water-colour – to
thread-bare all save
darkest

oils of sound

in sleep it

happens if you only get
half through a night
whose end is what

unwaking would have
made of it in mineshaft-
self by one death-flickered

lamp of trust you most
mornings wake to with
sash-white seeming all

but stashed between
static planes as life
stoushes with infant

fists against dying
light just at its flank
of thickening to start

into another day as strap-
hanger to myself grasping
blanks from which i rarely

lift the hidden eye
to ask am i yet a
wake? or better

– *do i not quite*
sleep? of sky in un
broken blue as if

death might come to
me fully lit or drowse
if i could stay with it

all that bitter way to
    cud some dawn steeped
        in juice or slumber whose

        point of breaking is
    almost that stunned
return to yesterday

i have stood

on spit of sand – water
forward & either
side – with

these feet
serous & barely
dissolving i looked

behind to tidal meniscus
there – deep into
turquoise

surge i
longed – on
three sides *extremitas*

inches out: sea peered
back at me – not
through

optics but
with organ of
light & muscular

intention (all clear under
moon more than sun
-bright) – i

neither sank
nor moved – this
recurs – depth forbidding

four sides (that moment i
step in to wake i
drown)

craning
to see life holds
less than shrunk &

shrinking headland – though
there never was time
i ventured by

night any s-
pit of sand & if
dreams of others send

us to sleep might
sea be some
thing near

-conscious
vastly & sleeping
that in its slumber dreams

me?

§

it is that loss

before the loss – glimpsed in
eye-glow of either while
still pressed

together – or as
air-hand grasp for child
lost to crowd while child still

trots beside you in blood
red duffel – or else
more acrid &

slow than *tock*
dropped smug from
wall of small hours he or

she has not yet phoned
or returned to – so
shall each re-

hearse grief
even while grief is
so far as to be thought

some crow shot skipping
down your field &
wingless toward

you: as though
the griefless prefer
that young & full-blown

parson hitching skirts black
with news he must
quickly yet

merely de-
liver & reaching
out half-mooned fingers

give – as he takes you
swooning by tip of
one elbow to

the other room

last word in the ward

was not one i could
take in your world or roll off
your slab or watch fall from you

as a petal from its vase – i
sought comforts instead
in longsighted science

its persistent ooze
down tubes or that sense
i had seen this – heard this all

before in public private places
hoping form so imitated by
sheets *was* you but you

at once introspective
as though some distant star
had need of your most absolute

attention – or that far-off bark
of street & shuffling of
leaves had th-

rust themselves up
one black root to which
your sap was due – so i wait

in your likeness for that far
gaze of breath – as one
must for grace or

something
said with which
to die: counting throat

a place where all winds
gather – thought their
engine generating

more space than re-
semblance whose words
work as stars in daylight or

rise in black ocean bringing
us with them to pop &
shudder the moon

of a face

that ward to which

i brought you dragging
hems of memory
& left you

among dreams
administered from
needle-ends as the doom

-mark crept along its chart &
all our future shrank
to furniture

unwanted fruit piled
brown upon deeper in its
po – till for good you went into

the machine – sank right
in as though you were
extension & i

followed neon-
green trace in place
of your eyes & bleep as if

it gave rise to breath & even
prayed to steady saline
rather than

hope for those
tears into which you
woke blinking with mouth

held open yet uncrying as i
laughed with unholy
quiet more like

father than son
seeing you born all
at once & so fully the

way the immaculate is
given to us or if not
given sent back

to this world

how flat these

mountains sc-
oured by planar base
of cloud – every sloping d-

own of pine to lower re-
aches become a
bubbling

blistering
verdigris patched
purpler with cemeteries

whose cypress bring thread-
worn corduroy to
listing

terraces as
each compulsion of
village encrusts its maternal

crease & through all this lull
of green the hospital
behind me s-

parse in its re-
petition of extinguishers
its under-swabbed faces & my

blood whose bedside i left for
brief air of valleys
that

hard face
of a woman still
mothering wan with an-

aesthetic beneath overdone sun
as skin ripples her
forearm

the way
lakewater herring-
bones outwards two ways in

fans overlapping – such
small flesh from a
summit whose

forehead
sleeps broad &
free from counterpaned

cloud
now con-
descending &

soon   soon
                        the eyes

i have heard in

dialect a kind of
phrase for it:
to *make a*

fall to
take a step
down to *slip back*

down – as though we
began with the
height of

ladders we
must descend
being told *never*

look between your
legs yet seeing
less as we

go unless
sight is same as
beginning to smell

earth & that sure
sense below
but

how
to resist if
it is my turn except

to hold firm in non-
resistance
as i

lower
myself between
narrow walls with their

ticking sounds &
watch my only
sky close

down to
meet you who
have last take on all

appointments – yet
i am still some
way up &

saw today
a snake black &
songless on a black

branch & not you down
there you kind im-
patient old

man – go
on waving your
stick & i shall shake

mine

motown

whose *vita* is
this woman in im-
possible heels & stood

right here inside my
blood & shapely
with the man i

am for whom
love is her face
novel behind that

mirrored frown – ah frame
on silvered frame each
take of light is what

my glance must
give her whose feline
dark in-forms me till death

bum-noted gets buried
to its bright-curved
back in lovema-

-king sound de-
siring my man-woman
hub against his tongue – that

nub of me brimming its *sapiens*
sap like a button in his
mouth – oh

death loves me
all-time & Waits to
make me all woman in

the pounding rain as rhythm finds
me & starts that knuckle-
clicking dance none

may finish till
led straight into his
arms & back knowing

no mountain high nor ocean
wide know *where*
to run no

where to hide

one pink heart

i ask – that & two grey
halves of sponge – if
wrong flesh must

take me let it have
head to sway me
full into what s-

wells within till b-
lack has clasped each
oilslick lung to put mere

breath in its coma &
nerves rewire to char of
cable & eyeballs grow sable

& stare through their irises :
two bone washers which c-
rack in dark but widen

to light – so ungradually
all of me going the
way of sloey pit

-uitary & black-o
-live testicle as hair
unthins to jet & turbo-

charged with black
turbans up for twice-
a-day clips i clop to on

charcoaled bones fis-
sured & more dee-
ply dark than sp-

ace on x-ray as order
-lies watch my blu-
shes rise japanned

(for even guarded
smile shows molars set
under livered tongue like b-

lackcurrant gums)
& still they help me
nurse each massive black

-bean kidney as if it were
their own & wipe mole
-flesh arse spotting &

spreading then joining my
whole skin over though
i wont mind so long

as i make an ink of
blood *oh* ill walk that
negative self down the

road invisible against
asphalt – this old body t-
urned antimatter ganger &

all honest tumour except
for will in its two b-
right halves &

under its rib that un-
stoppable fib-
rillant

muscle

watch all weathers for

i am no
sack of kitten-
bone time must dr-

own nor emptying gourd
of venous potentials
but cumulo

-nimbus cr-
ouched with self
-weight & forging sky

with you who touch & in
touching precipitate
between these

sheets of walking-
earth we rut a making
of sense & resonant by

me stand to see me stand
beside myself in
freedom

no formula
but enough life to
choke on – oh if i in

deed *am* gone let me kiss
each clay lip you
walk – for

i continue
in every gaze you
mazed into me as thought s-

hot through us till each
form of me cannot
fail recalling

your turning
look : as if lifting
eyes at last to night

you saw not dark but
one cloud drift
behind

its moon

in loss these hands

work my lap
as if they belong
to another : at height-

grief this small-beaked
heart strains to de-
part ribs as

though start-
led at window-self
by its flight & when

endings flower too
close & dark i
watch me

walk round
– yet am not
body but space

this travelling not-yet
that opens before me
into whose harness

i step & where
they are : the dead i
know & the dead i am

to become – are
that in which i
move but

never arrive

"Let no fruit grow on thee. . ."

& when he came to it

it was in spate – as though
a river green with
swelling had

halted & stood
up in itself or some
white sea had swung there

a green hull creaking
with its swell of
fruit & he
-

stood in that
wide shade hungered
seeing side by side two

purpled fruit blushed &
strained with summer
he took them

split them
drank that sweetness
of a tree so long expectant

as one gold drop slunk
from his lip it came
upon him so

deep he moved
away from them &
leaning forward rested

one smooth palm on that
smooth grey trunk
& swallowing

his half
-seeded curse for two
moments & with all before him

forgot himself

we have to talk you &

you – come starred
space   sit at yourself
: these two black stars

glump eyes &
talk as though suns
never scorched that solar

plexus into the anon
i am that turns its satellite
dish of face to night as if your

Very pole might cast
some received incoming
weakness : signal some limen

to overture sense
where none is   a pencil
of yeses from one infinitely

far to another for
if you are thus from me i
must be from you who blind-

seeing through primal
shush of waves break their
reddened monotony on shores of

aided eye as b-
rushing photonic rand-
omness never stills its flicker-tongued

energy you make
me what you will &
i give it back as good

cramming you
headlong as   you
come into skull so

crania before mine
aligned their bone abacus
compass-balls that spun to your

magnetic truth soon
buried as part-receivers to
cement layers no more significant

than any previous
carboniferous squib   so
speak then – as though all life

depended from
it utter while irrefutable
make some micro-shock   some

chordotonal any
-sex tremor my furthest
reaches as atlantic whales might sense

our atom
bombed in bikini to thrust
meaning into this lowered-for-love gut or god

as zest so it
-self as to halve my probing
tongue or your close-conscious scintilla tobogganing

my one-whorled
fingertip-galaxy watched
to extinction or that glance caught in your last

mirror to spot me
face-down in the river whose
lop-sided black makes me wave to you as i

go down as all
my digits go mackling
down   through black milt that ought to

buoy me
ipsissimum & how i
ail & hud & shuck each part of me

whose weeds are
hair ready to whiten & un-
bereave   who swap bearings

x for y for zimmer as
words recede to backwoods
sounds trying to commute into

-ne what you have
ever been more parlous
than speaking freighted with

silence which is
nothing in flux
as music is

means within
its scale – so go
you all buccal & s-

trap trailing logic & its
misdemeanours as cynosure
seeking the trine we two must point to

i seedless on
my cob without you my
dendron bod made dottle of smoke among your

stacks those
fumarole fastnesses   your ec-
crisis of elements that stink & charge &

chain electric
conversations until
i must be quietus seeing this

nonce self
speaking from
behind a jalousie world

od to your ossa
though your mashmatter
morning to morning endlessly

rewarms in me
this yellow-white fat of torso
kerf to my tree as i swing for you

dry as kex   never
quite free to talk war
& love or whisper

ultima   i have missed you i
have   as even with
last breaths

id want you starred &
talking any three
words either

i love you
it is finished
but choose or else

look down for me
as i last-breathe
you   i am

my own rood

so

will i
be not where i
am to go nor where i

was but all night between
whose sum we are
as two di-

urnal
turn to one rain
rinsing rain into each

I